Who's Who
in a
School Community

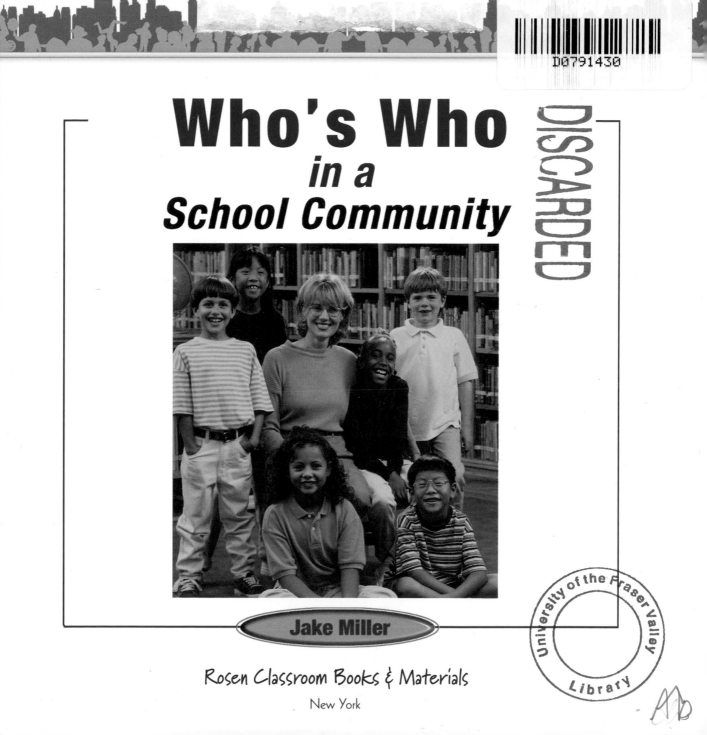

Jake Miller

Rosen Classroom Books & Materials

New York

Published in 2005 by The Rosen Publishing Group, Inc.
29 East 21st Street, New York, NY 10010

First Edition

Editor: Joanne Randolph
Book Design: Maria E. Melendez
Layout Design: Emily Muschinske

Photo Credits: Cover and p. 1 © Jose Luis Pelaez, Inc./CORBIS; p. 5 © Patrick Bennett/CORBIS; pp. 7, 9 © Ed Bock/CORBIS; p. 11 © Jim Cummins/CORBIS; p. 13 © Tom Stewart/CORBIS; p. 15 © Gabe Palmer/CORBIS; p. 17 © Richard T. Nowitz/CORBIS; p. 19 © Richard Hutchings/CORBIS; p. 21 © Ronnie Kaufman/CORBIS.

Library of Congress Cataloging-in-Publication Data

Miller, Jake, 1969–
Who's who in a school community / Jake Miller.
    p. cm. — (Communities at work)
Includes bibliographical references (p.   ) and index.
ISBN 1-4042-2788-1 (Library Binding) – ISBN 1-4042-5030-1 (pbk.)
1. School employees—Juvenile literature. 2. Students—Juvenile literature. 3. Schools—Juvenile literature. [1. School employees. 2. Schools.] I. Title. II. Series.
LB2831.5.M47 2005
371—dc22

                              2003024814

Manufactured in the United States of America

Contents

Working Together at School

A **community** is a group of people who spend time together and share a place. They usually try to help each other.

Communities can be as big as a whole city or as small as one family. Schools are one kind of community. Many people are part of a school community.

A teacher greets students as they enter the school. Teachers and students are both important parts of the school community. ▷

COMMUNITY NEWS

There are many different kinds of schools. There are elementary schools for young children. Middle schools teach older children. High schools and colleges teach young adults and adults.

The Heart of the School

You could not have a school without students. Schools are built so that students have a place to learn. Students learn many different **subjects** in school. They learn to read, write, and do math. They also learn how to get along with other children and with their teachers.

Here a student is pointing to the country of India on a map. Learning how to read a map is an important skill. ▷

The Student Body

All the students in a school are called the student **body**. There can be a lot of students in one school. There can be a lot of students in each **grade**, too.

Students are usually put together in classes. Usually they are placed in classes with students in their own grade. That way one teacher can teach many students at once.

Sometimes a class will have the same teacher all day long. Other classes move from room to room. They study different subjects with different teachers.

COMMUNITY NEWS

Many students sit at their own desks in class. In some classes, students sit in a circle on the floor. In other classes students may go outside to learn about trees or grass.

What Teachers Do

A teacher is an important part of the school community. The teacher helps students to learn. Each student in a classroom is different. The teacher must find a way to help all the different students to understand what is taught. This is a hard job!

The teacher asks questions during class to find out if students are learning. ▷

COMMUNITY NEWS

A principal works for a person called the superintendent. Usually the superintendent is in charge of many different schools in a town or an area. The superintendent makes sure that each principal has what he or she needs to do a good job.

The Leader of the School

The **principal** is the leader of the school community. She or he is in charge of running the school. The principal makes sure that the teachers have everything they need for teaching. The principal makes sure that the students have everything they need for learning.

Sometimes students bother other kids. The principal reminds them to be nice. She or he chooses new teachers. Sometimes the principal even picks the menu for the lunchroom.

The Librarian

The **librarian** is part of the school community. He or she is in charge of the library. The librarian helps students and teachers find **information**. The librarian orders books, videos, and **magazines** for the library. He or she puts these things in the right place so that they are easy to find.

This librarian is helping a student to find information in a book. If the library does not have a book, the librarian can get it from another library. ▷

Health and Safety

The school nurse has many different jobs. Students can get sick or hurt. The nurse helps them feel better. He or she can decide if the student needs to go home or to the doctor.

The nurse can help students to take **medicine**. He or she also makes sure that all the students have had their **immunizations**.

This nurse is helping a student who does not feel well. Sometimes the school nurse teaches health classes. That way students learn how to stay healthy.

Balanced Meals

Lunchroom workers are another part of the school community. Students need to eat a **nutritious** meal at school. The food keeps their minds working hard. The lunchroom worker cooks and serves lunch to the students. He or she makes sure that the food is prepared in a way that is healthy and tasty.

Here a lunchroom worker serves a student lunch. The lunchroom worker has an important job in the school community. Students need healthy meals to help them to do well in class.

The Way to School

Some students ride the bus to and from school. The bus driver picks them up at their house or at a bus stop in the morning. He or she drops them off again when school gets out. Other children walk to school. A crossing guard may help them to cross busy streets on the way to school. The people who help students to get to school are part of the school community.

A crossing guard helps students to cross the street. That way parents do not have to worry about their children getting to school safely. ▷

Everybody Has a Part to Play

Teachers, principals, bus drivers, parents, lunchroom workers, and **custodians** are all important parts of the school community. They help students to learn. Students have a job to do, too. They follow the rules to help make school a safe, healthy place. The whole school community works together to make school a place where everyone can learn to be his or her best.

Glossary

body (BAH-dee) A whole group together.

community (kuh-MYOO-nih-tee) A place where people live and work together, or the people who make up such a place.

custodians (kuh-STOH-dee-unz) People in charge of keeping a building or other place clean and in good shape.

grade (GRAYD) A year or a class in school.

immunizations (ih-myoo-nih-ZAY-shunz) Shots that keep you from getting sick.

information (in-fer-MAY-shun) Facts, figures, stories, pictures, and numbers.

librarian (ly-BRER-ee-en) The person in charge of the library. The library is a place where people go to get books, magazines, and videos.

magazines (MA-guh-zeenz) Printed stories and articles that are usually grouped and held together by a paper cover.

medicine (MEH-duh-sin) A drug that a doctor gives you to help fight illness.

nutritious (noo-TRIH-shus) Full of things the body needs to stay healthy.

principal (PRIN-seh-pul) The person who is the head of a school.

subjects (SUB-jekts) Different things to study, such as art, reading, music, or math.

Index

Web Sites

Due to the changing nature of Internet links, PowerKids Press has developed an online list of Web sites related to the subject of this book. This site is updated regularly. Please use this link to access the list:
www.powerkidslinks.com/caw/whoscom/